Did Yo

LON

A MISCELLANY

Compiled by Julia Skinner

With particular reference to the work of Martin Andrew,
Leigh Hatts and Terence Sackett

THE FRANCIS FRITH COLLECTION

www.francisfrith.com

First published in the United Kingdom in 2011 by The Francis Frith Collection®

This edition published exclusively for Identity Books in 2012 ISBN 978-1-84589-570-9

British Library Cataloguing in Publication Data

Did You Know? London - A Miscellany
Compiled by Julia Skinner
With particular reference to the work of Martin Andrew, Leigh Hatts and Terence Sackett

The Francis Frith Collection
Oakley Business Park,
Wylye Road, Dinton,
Wiltshire SP3 5EU
Tel: +44 (0) 1722 716 376
Email: info@francisfrith.co.uk
www.francisfrith.com

Printed and bound in Malaysia

Front Cover: **LONDON, PARLIAMENT SQUARE 1890**   L130008p
Frontispiece: **LONDON, THE CLOCK TOWER AND WESTMINSTER BRIDGE c1890**
L130182

The colour-tinting is for illustrative purposes only, and is not intended to be historically accurate

CONTENTS

INTRODUCTION

Sweet Thames, run softly, till I end my song!

(From 'Prothalamion', Edmund Spenser, 1552-1599)

The River Thames which flows through London was the reason for the city's foundation in the first century AD, when the Romans established a trading port called 'Londinium' beside the river. Londinium became the largest settlement in the Roman province of 'Britannia', and eventually its capital. A defensive wall around the city was built between AD190 and AD225, parts of which can still be seen at the Barbican, in the north of the City of London. The Museum of London near the Barbican Centre holds many Roman finds that have been excavated in the city and has permanent Roman exhibitions.

The Romans left Britain in the fifth century, and Londonium fell into decline; it became almost deserted, and the Roman public buildings fell into ruin. Then in the Anglo Saxon period a new trading settlement called 'Lundenwic' ('London Market') was established a mile upstream from the walled Roman city, in what is now the Covent Garden, Strand and Aldwych area. Lundenwic prospered, but repeated Viking attacks eventually forced the inhabitants to move back to the old Roman walled city for protection. In the ninth century the Anglo-Saxon King Alfred the Great made peace with the Vikings and restored the city, and its fortunes revived; the Alfred Plaque near Southwark Bridge commemorates his achievements. By the tenth century, London was an international port with wharves and warehouses along the river. Thereafter London thrived and prospered. By the late 18th century it was the world's busiest port, and the London Docks were built to cope with the trade. In the 19th century the extensive docks of the Pool of London became the busiest and wealthiest in human history. Great ships plied the estuary of the Thames to docks as far upriver as London Bridge, and stevedores and dock workers loaded and unloaded coal, timber, and all manner of exports and exotic imports.

Until the end of the 18th century London was a compact city. Its merchants lived in the historic core of London known as 'the City', and the aristocracy in fashionable areas like Piccadilly and the West End. However, in the 19th century London grew at an extraordinary rate. The City developed into the centre of world finance, London's burgeoning banks and insurance companies clamoured for space in the overcrowded city, and new streets of Victorian Gothic offices were constructed where armies of clerks and office workers came to work each day. Neighbourhoods of old ramshackle buildings were demolished and the great thoroughfares we know today were created; much of the West End was remodelled, and great houses and mansions were constructed; and magnificent public spaces such as Trafalgar Square and Piccadilly Circus were created and embellished by public sculpture and memorials. By the end of the 19th century, London's beautiful streets and buildings had earned it a reputation as one of the great cities of the world.

Most of the photographs in this book show London in the Victorian period, before the city suffered terrible damage and loss of life during the Second World War. Between September 1940 and May 1941 London was bombed for 57 successive nights, an era known as 'the Blitz'. Enemy action destroyed many buildings in the City and devastated the East End, where the docks, railways and industry of this part of London formed a target for enemy bombing. The rebuilding programme after the war dramatically altered much of the landscape of the city, and the process is still continuing today, with some stunning modern structures standing proudly in the skyline alongside older historic buildings. One of the most interesting is City Hall, the headquarters of the Greater London Authority (GLA), which was designed in an unusual bulbous shape to reduce its surface area and improve energy efficiency. Nicknamed 'The Onion', it stands at Southwark on the south bank of the Thames, the river that caused this great city to be founded almost 2,000 years ago.

COCKNEY RHYMING SLANG

According to tradition, a Londoner born within earshot of the bells of the church of St Mary-le-Bow in Cheapside is known as a Cockney. The meaning of the term 'Cockney' is now lost in time, but London is famous for its Cockney culture, which includes favourite dishes such as jellied eels and pie and mash, and the 'Pearly Kings and Queens' who wear clothing decorated with intricate patterns of pearl buttons and raise money for London charities. Cockney culture is also famous for its 'rhyming slang' which originated from the East End in the 19th century, perhaps as a way of allowing market traders to talk secretly amongst themselves, or perhaps as an amusing local way of talking which helped maintain a sense of community. The principle of Cockney rhyming slang involves replacing the word for something with a phrase of two or three words, the last word of which rhymes with the original subject word; then the original subject word is omitted, making the origin and meaning of the phrase elusive to listeners not in the know. Here are some examples of phrases in common usage:

'Dog and bone' – telephone.

'Trouble and strife' – wife.

'China plate' – mate (thus 'me old china').

'Plates of meat' – feet.

'Frog and toad' – road.

'Barnet Fair' – hair.

'Butcher's hook' – look (thus 'have a butcher's' for 'have a look').

'Britney Spears' – beers.

'Loaf of bread' – head (thus 'use your loaf' for 'use your brain').

'Sweeney Todd' – the 'Flying Squad', a rapid response unit of London's Metropolitan Police, also known as 'The Sweeney'.

HAUNTED LONDON

With such a long, eventful history it is not surprising that London is full of places reputed to be haunted. Here are two of the city's most famous 'haunted pubs':

The Morpeth Arms sits on a corner site at 58 Millbank, Westminster (SW1P 4RW), overlooking the River Thames near Vauxhall Bridge. The pub is built on part of the site of the old Millbank Prison, which was demolished in the 1890s. The prison had accommodation for around 1,200 prisoners, and in the basement beneath the pub are some of the old, cramped cells where they were incarcerated. The Morpeth Arms is reputed to be haunted by the ghost of a prisoner who was held in the cells and died there whilst he was waiting to be transported to Australia – the convict ships docked just outside where the pub now stands, to take on board the prisoners from the gaol.

Possibly the most famous haunted pub in London is The Grenadier in Belgravia, hidden away in Wilton Row, located just behind Wilton Crescent, to the north of Belgrave Square (SW1X 7NR). Wilton Row is a former mews (row of stables) which used to be part of the barracks of the Duke of Wellington's guards – the 'Iron Duke', victor of the battle of Waterloo in 1815, lived nearby in Apsley House at Hyde Park Corner. The upper floor of The Grenadier was used as the officers' mess. According to the tale, one day a young subaltern was caught cheating at cards in the mess. His comrades flogged him so severely for his dishonourable behaviour that he died as a result, and his unhappy shade is said to have haunted the building ever since. A great deal of paranormal activity seems to occur there, including the sound of disembodied footsteps in empty rooms, and strange moaning sounds coming from the cellar. Objects are mysteriously moved around or disappear, and tables and chairs sometimes appear to be rattled by an unseen hand…

LONDON MISCELLANY

One of the most famous buildings in the city is the Tower of London, actually a complex of several buildings set within defensive walls. The White Tower, which gives the entire castle its name, was completed in 1078 by order of William the Conqueror. The Tower of London has fulfilled many functions over the centuries, including use as a prison and arsenal as well as a royal residence. It has a dark history, and many terrible and tragic events have taken place there, including the mysterious disappearance of the 'Princes in the Tower', Edward V (born 1470) and Richard, Duke of York (born 1473), the two sons of Edward IV who were kept prisoner in the tower by their uncle Richard III after he usurped the throne; Richard III is believed to have ordered the princes to be murdered in the Tower in 1483, and in 1674 the skeletons of two children were discovered under a staircase in the White Tower, which may be their remains. This photograph shows the pinnacles of the White Tower piercing the sky, with the waters of the Thames lapping at the water-gate known as Traitors Gate, through which prisoners accused of treason passed after being brought along the river by barge. Often their journey would take them past London Bridge where the heads of recently executed traitors were displayed on pikes, and where their own might soon be on show...

Tower Green in the precincts of the Tower is where some famous names in history met their deaths by execution, including two of Henry VIII's wives, Anne Boleyn and Katherine Howard. There is now a modern memorial on Tower Green to all those executed there by order of the State. Around it is a poem composed by the artist, Brian Catling, which reads: 'Gentle visitor pause awhile: where you stand death cut away the light of many days: here jewelled names were broken from the vivid thread of life: may they rest in peace while we walk the generations around their strife and courage: under these restless skies'.

The Crown Jewels are kept in the Jewel House of the Tower of London. They include the magnificent Imperial State Crown, adorned with 2,868 diamonds, 273 pearls, 17 sapphires, 11 emeralds and 5 rubies, which is worn by the monarch at the State Opening of Parliament each year.

The Yeoman Warders who stand guard at the Tower in their distinctive uniforms are recruited from the armed forces after serving for at least 22 years. The Yeomen Warders are popularly known as Beefeaters, which probably derives from when they used to be paid part of their salary with portions of meat. Nowadays, the 'real' beefeaters at the Tower are the famous ravens that live there; the large black birds are carnivorous and are fed on a daily allowance of raw meat. Ravens have lived at the Tower of London for centuries, giving rise to an old legend that 'If the ravens ever leave the Tower, the kingdom will fall'. They are cared for by the Ravenmaster to make sure they are happy enough at the Tower not to leave and put the legend to the test!

LONDON, THE TOWER OF LONDON c1950 L1305022

The correct name for Westminster Abbey is the Collegiate Church of St Peter, but in the 11th century it became known as 'west minster' to distinguish it from the nearby 'east minster' of St Paul's Cathedral. This sublime abbey is one of Britain's most famous religious buildings. In the 13th century Henry III (1207-1272) began the reshaping of Edward the Confessor's old church which was built around 1045-50, rebuilding it in French Gothic style. Restyling continued until well into the 16th century. One of the most important additions to the abbey was the Henry VII Chapel at its east end, built by Henry VII (1457-1509), the first Tudor king, and completed in 1512. It is the burial place of Henry VII and his wife, Elizabeth of York. The effigies of Henry and his wife on their monument are Italian Renaissance in style (by Pietro Torrigiani), an extremely early example in England.

In the 18th century the west front of the abbey was embellished by its twin towers, designed in medieval style by Nicholas Hawksmoor, and completed in 1745. In the 1990s the figures of 20th-century martyrs, including Martin Luther King and Oscar Romero, were added to the empty niches above the west door of the abbey.

Westminster Abbey has been the setting for many royal weddings and coronations – all but two of the English kings and queens since William I, 'the Conqueror', in 1066 have been crowned there. The Abbey is also the final resting place of many famous people, including Elizabeth I and her sister, Mary I, and also Mary Queen of Scots. The area known as 'Poets Corner' in the south transept is the burial place of illustrious writers, playwrights and poets, many famous musicians are buried in the 'Musicians Aisle' (the north choir aisle), and the Statesmen's Aisle in the north transept is where a number of great names from British history lie at peace. However, one of the most poignant tombs in the abbey is that of the Unknown Warrior in the nave, which commemorates all those who died in the First World War (1914-18) who have no other memorial or known grave.

LONDON,
WESTMINSTER
ABBEY c1867
L130142

9

The 'City of London' is the name for a small area in central London which is the historic core around which the modern metropolis grew. In the medieval period, this was the full extent of London. In the distance of the photograph on the opposite page, the spire of the church of St Mary-le-Bow in Cheapside soars over the City. The present church was rebuilt after the medieval church was destroyed in the Great Fire of London in 1666. In medieval times Bow Bells rang the nightly curfew for the citizens of London, and it is traditionally asserted that the only true Londoner is one born within earshot of the bells. The building with a portico on the left of the photograph is the Mansion House, which has been the official residence of the Lord Mayor of London for two centuries. A famous name from medieval London is Richard (Dick) Whittington, who came to the city from Gloucestershire, became a successful and wealthy cloth mercer and served as Mayor of London four times, in 1397, 1398, 1406 and 1419. Although his story has been embellished over the centuries, and he is best-known nowadays as a pantomime character assisted to success by a magical cat, he was a real person. He used his wealth to finance a number of public projects in London, and after his death in 1423 he bequeathed his fortune to form the Charity of Sir Richard Whittington, which still assists those in need. Dick Whittington made a number of endowments to the medieval church of St Michael Paternoster Royal, near Cannon Street Station, which contains a stained glass memorial window to him, and he is remembered in the name of the Whittington Hospital on Highgate Hill in north London, traditionally the place where the sound of Bow Bells encouraged him to turn back to London to try his luck again when he had given up hope of making his fortune and was on his way home. There is also a monument to him on Highgate Hill, The Whittington Stone, which features his legendary cat.

LONDON, MANSION HOUSE AND CHEAPSIDE c1890 L130177

The above photograph shows the 1890's view west down Poultry which leads directly into Cheapside, once the site of one of the principal produce markets in London – 'cheap' meant 'market' in medieval English. Many of the streets feeding into Cheapside are named after the produce sold in those areas of the market in the Middle Ages, such as Honey Lane, Milk Street, Bread Street, Poultry and Cornhill.

Those who look upwards from London's bustling streets will often find unusual features on the buildings. On a Victorian office building opposite St Peter's Church in Cornhill, on the corner with Gracechurch Street, 'the three devils of Cornhill' glower down on the world below. In the 19th century, when the building was just about to be erected, the vicar of the church spotted that the plans for the structure intruded by one foot (30cms) on to the church's property. He made an official objection, and the architect had to re-draw his plans. In revenge, the architect designed these three terracotta devils to adorn the building, facing the church, and apparently, one of them bears a distinct resemblance to the vicar who scuppered his original plans!

On the exterior of number 13 Philpot Lane on the eastern side of the City, between Eastcheap and Fenchurch Street, is a small sculpture depicting two mice fighting over a piece of cheese. The story goes that when the building was constructed in the 17th century, one of the workmen accused another of eating his food; the men fought, and one fell to his death from the scaffolding. It was later realised that mice were the culprits, and this sculpture was added to the fascia of the building as a memorial of the tragedy.

One of the few surviving medieval churches in the City of London is St Olave's Church in Hart Street, which narrowly escaped destruction in the Great Fire of London in 1666; it is the burial place of Samuel Pepys, who provided a graphic eye-witness account of the Great Fire in his famous diaries, and who worshipped there. St Olave's Church is famous for the macabre entrance arch to its churchyard from Seething Lane, crowned with a cluster of skulls carved from stone; this dates from 1658 and serves as a 'Memento Mori'. This churchyard has a sad place in London's history, for it is said to be the burial place of Mary Ramsay, the woman reputed to have brought the bubonic plague to London that killed up to 100,000 people between 1665-66, which was also chronicled by Samuel Pepys. On a lighter note, a plaque outside the church commemorates the internment in the churchyard in 1586 of an eccentric London character called 'Old Mother Goose', who used to knit little boots for her geese to protect their feet as they were herded to market.

The Great Fire of London started on the night of September 2nd 1666 in a bakery in Pudding Lane and quickly swept through the wooden buildings of the old city. The blaze raged for four days, consuming most of the old buildings and landmarks of medieval London. It was estimated that around 70,000 of the city's 80,000 inhabitants had lost their homes, and Samuel Pepys described the devastated city as 'the saddest sight of desolation that I ever saw'.

As part of the rebuilding of London after the Great Fire, a memorial of the conflagration was erected at the junction of Monument Street and Fish Street Hill. The Doric column is 202 feet (61.5 metres) high – the distance between the monument and Pudding Lane where the fire started – and is topped with a gilded sculpture depicting an urn from which flames are emerging. The Fire Monument is open to the public, who can climb up the 311 steps inside to a viewing platform to enjoy a panoramic view of the city. The tall column of the Monument is seen in the background of photograph L130317 (below) of London Bridge, which connects the City of London with Southwark, on the south bank of the Thames. The current London Bridge opened in 1973 and is the most recent structure in a succession of bridges to claim that name. The London Bridge seen in this photograph was completed in 1831, replacing the 12th-century one of nursery rhyme fame which had lasted for over six centuries. Demolished in 1968, the London Bridge in this view was re-erected in the USA at Lake Huvasu City in Arizona.

LONDON, LONDON BRIDGE c1900 L130317

The Great Fire of 1666 reduced London's old medieval St Paul's Cathedral to a virtual ruin, and in 1668 the architect Sir Christopher Wren was commissioned to design a new cathedral. The magnificent building that Wren produced, perched on the summit of Ludgate Hill at almost the highest point in the City, is the pride of London. St Paul's Cathedral is in the form of a cross, built in the Corinthian style, and surmounted by the giant dome which rises on arches over the centre, which is one of the most famous landmarks of London's skyline.

The famous Whispering Gallery of St Paul's Cathedral runs round the vault of the huge Dome where it starts to curve inwards. The curve of the Dome at this point causes a special acoustic effect, so that the sound of someone quietly whispering on one side of the Dome can clearly be heard by another person on the opposite side, as the sound carries around the vast circular gallery.

Many great men and women are buried in St Paul's Cathedral, including its architect, Sir Christopher Wren, in his masterpiece. On the wall above his grave in the south aisle at the east end of the Crypt is inscribed 'Lector, si monumentum requires, circumspice' – 'Reader, if you seek his monument, look around you'.

Also in the Crypt of the cathedral is the magnificent tomb of the naval hero Admiral Lord Nelson, who was killed on his flagship the 'Victory' during the battle of Trafalgar in 1805. This Renaissance sarcophagus was originally commissioned by Cardinal Wolsey, the powerful churchman and political figure of Henry VIII's reign, to be used for his own tomb at Windsor after his death. However, Wolsey fell from favour with Henry VIII, and after his death in 1530 he was buried in an unmarked grave in St Mary's Abbey in Leicester where he had died. His impressive black monument was left in a storeroom at Windsor until it was brought out to be used for Nelson's state funeral in 1806.

To the north of St Paul's Cathedral, between Little Britain and Angel Street, is a peaceful space known as Postman's Park because it was once a favourite lunchtime spot for workers from the General Post Office which used to be nearby. A moving and decorative feature of the park is a wall created by the Victorian artist and sculptor George F Watts as a memorial to local people who died whilst they were trying to save the lives of others. Their bravery is commemorated with a tiled plaque on the wall in memory of each person, detailing their heroic act.

A relic of London's earliest times can be found in Cannon Street in the City of London. Opposite the main entrance to Cannon Street Station is the London Stone, which is said to be the place from which the Romans measured all distances from their town of Londinium in their province of Britannia. For many years in the Middle Ages the London Stone was recognised as the symbolic authority and heart of the City of London, where deals were forged, oaths were sworn and from where official proclamations were made.

LONDON, ST PAUL'S CATHEDRAL c1860 L130282

LONDON, THE BANK OF ENGLAND AND THE ROYAL EXCHANGE
c1910 L130207

The historic area known as the 'City of London' is often referred to as the 'City', or the 'Square Mile', as it covers an area of just over one square mile. The UK's banking and financial services industries have historically been based there. London's Royal Exchange was founded in 1565 by Sir Thomas Gresham as a centre of commerce. His original building was destroyed in the Great Fire in 1666, and its successor was itself replaced by the magnificent building seen in the photograph above, which opened for trading in 1845. The pediment features sculpted figures representing Commerce holding the charter of the Exchange, attended by the Lord Mayor and merchants. The Royal Exchange ceased to act as a centre of commerce in 1939 and the building is now a luxurious shopping centre. However, a reminder of its original function remains on the cupola on the roof, which is surmounted by a weathervane in the form of a large golden grasshopper. This commemorates Sir Thomas Gresham, the 16th-century founder of the Royal Exchange, whose family crest featured a grasshopper.

The Temple area of the City is named after the 12th-century Temple Church that was built there for the Knights Templar, a Christian military order of the Middle Ages linked with the Crusades. The Templar Church is famous for its effigy tombs and for its original nave section, called the Round Church, which was constructed on a round design based on the Church of the Holy Sepulchre in Jerusalem. The church featured in the novel 'The Da Vinci Code' by Dan Brown, and was also used as a location in the film of that book.

The photograph below shows the imposing gateway of Temple Bar in 1875, in its original position at the west end of Fleet Street where it marked the western boundary of the City of London. Temple Bar was erected there in 1672, but by the 1870s it was causing traffic congestion; it was taken down and Sir Henry Meux had it re-erected as a gate to his estate at Theobalds in Hertfordshire. In 2003, Temple Bar was taken down again and re-erected in Paternoster Square in London, near St Paul's Cathedral. The project was completed in November 2004.

LONDON, TEMPLE BAR 1875 L130141

The Clerkenwell area of London is named after the historic Clerks' Well, part of which is incorporated into a building called Well Court in Farringdon Lane, visible through a window of the building. In later centuries the area was known as 'Little Italy' because many Italian immigrants settled there. The 19th-century author Charles Dickens knew the area well, and in his novel 'Oliver Twist', Fagin and the Artful Dodger inducted Oliver into pickpocketing amongst shoppers in the busy market at Clerkenwell Green.

The thoroughfare of Holborn which links the City with the West End takes its name from the Oldbourne Bridge which once spanned the Fleet River after which Fleet Street is named (the river now flows underground). On the south side of High Holborn, opposite the junction with Gray's Inn Road, is the 16th-century Staple Inn, so called because it was once the meeting place for wool merchants with a custom house where wool dues and taxes, 'the wool staple', were collected. This photograph shows Staple Inn in the 1870s, before the plaster rendering had been stripped off to reveal the magnificent frontage of half-timbered work that is seen today.

LONDON, STAPLE INN c1875 L130136

**LONDON, PORTSMOUTH STREET, THE OLD CURIOSITY SHOP
c1875** L130121

South of High Holborn is another historic building, shown in
photograph L130121, above. This quaint old house, built around 1570,
sits on a corner site on Portsmouth Street, just off Lincoln's Inn Fields,
where it is dwarfed by neighbouring tall, modern buildings. It is said
to be both London's oldest shop and to have been the inspiration for
Charles Dickens as the home of Little Nell and her grandfather in his
novel 'The Old Curiosity Shop'. The building still functions as a shop,
protected by a preservation order.

South of Lincoln's Inn Fields is Aldwych. The name of Aldwych derives
from the name of 'Ealdwic', meaning 'the old market' of the old Anglo-
Saxon trading settlement called 'Lundenwic' that was established in
this area in the early 7th century, some distance away from the earlier
Roman walled city of Londinium.

North-west of Alwych is the Covent Garden area, with its magnificent central square designed by Inigo Jones in the 17th century in Italian arcaded style. London's most important fruit, vegetable and flower markets for the area north of the Thames used to be located in Covent Garden. The market porters carried goods to waiting carts in tower blocks of circular baskets on their heads, and took pride in the number they could carry. The produce distribution market has now moved to the New Covent Garden Market a few miles away at Nine Elms, and the square (or Covent Garden Piazza) is now a shopping and tourist site famous for its street entertainers, who have to audition and are then given timetabled slots. The first recorded Punch and Judy puppet show in Britain took place in Covent Garden in May 1662; the marionette show featuring an early version of the Mr Punch character was performed by an Italian puppet showman and watched by Samuel Pepys, who described it in his diary as 'an Italian puppet play, that is within the rails there, which is very pretty'.

LONDON, COVENT GARDEN 1900 L130026A

LONDON, THE STRAND AND CHARING CROSS 1890 L130180

The Strand stretches from Temple Bar to Trafalgar Square in the West End and was originally the waterside thoroughfare between the City and Westminster – 'strand' means 'shoreline'. This photograph shows the Strand at the Trafalgar Square end, where the Victorian replica 'Eleanor Cross' stands outside Charing Cross station. The original medieval Eleanor Cross, destroyed in 1647, was sited where the equestrian statue of King Charles I now stands at the south of Trafalgar Square, looking towards the spot in Whitehall where he was executed in 1649 during the Civil War. It was one of the commemorative crosses erected by King Edward I to mark where the funeral cortege of his beloved wife Queen Eleanor stopped for the night whilst bringing her body to London for burial in Westminster Abbey after her death in Lincoln in 1291. It is often said that the name of Charing Cross comes from the French 'chère reine', or 'dear queen', but this is not true – 'Charing' comes from the old word 'cierring', referring to a nearby bend in the Thames, which was the name of this area in medieval times.

LONDON, TRAFALGAR SQUARE 1890 L130190

Trafalgar Square was created in the 1830s. Its name commemorates Admiral Lord Nelson's naval victory over the French at the battle of Trafalgar in 1805, during the Napoleonic Wars. The centrepiece of the square is Nelson's column, 170 feet (52 metres) high and topped off with a massive statue of Lord Nelson. The four immense crouching bronze lions by Landseer that guard the foot of the memorial were added in the 1860s. The bronze bas-reliefs at the base of the column are cast from cannons captured in Nelson's naval battles.

At Christmas time a giant Christmas tree is erected in Trafalgar Square, which is given annually by the people of Norway as a remembrance of British help to their country in the Second World War.

In the centre of the photograph on pages 22-23, by the steps down to the lower level of the Square, is the equestrian statue of George IV, who was Prince Regent at the time of the battle of Trafalgar. Commissioned in 1829, it was originally planned to go on top of Marble Arch, which then stood in front of Buckingham Palace, but was set up in Trafalgar Square in 1843. It is in Classical style, showing the king dressed as a Roman emperor. The domed, porticoed building on the left hand side of the photograph is the National Gallery which houses the national collection of Western European painting from the 13th to the 19th centuries. Erected in the 1830s, the long frontage of the National Gallery was extended further to the west in 1991 by the ingenious Sainsbury Wing, a notable example of Postmodernist architecture in which classical columns and features gradually die out. The building with the spire in the background of the photograph is James Gibbs' wonderful 1720s' church of St-Martin-in-the-Fields, famous for its work among London's homeless which has given it the epithet 'The Church of the Ever Open Door'. It is also renowned for its music, and is the home of the Academy of St Martin in the Fields, a chamber music orchestra.

Whitehall runs south of Trafalgar Square into Parliament Street and is the traditional home of the offices of government, including the Treasury, Home Office and Privy Council. In the middle of Whitehall is the Cenotaph, the national war memorial that is the focus of the Remembrance Day parade every November. Just past the Cenotaph is the entrance to Downing Street, where 'Number 10' is the official residence of the Prime Minister. Originally three houses, 'Number 10' contains around 100 rooms used for residential, office and reception purposes, where national leaders and foreign dignitaries are met and entertained. Whitehall was once the site of Whitehall Palace, but the only substantial remnant is the Banqueting House, famous for the magnificent painted ceiling in the main hall by Sir Peter Paul Rubens, installed in 1636. The Palladian-style Horse Guards in Whitehall was built in the 1750s on the site of the Guard House of Whitehall Palace, and is the oldest purpose-built barracks in England. From 10am to 4pm Horse Guards is guarded by two mounted Troopers of the Household Cavalry, who are relieved every hour.

LONDON, WHITEHALL, HORSE GUARDS c1960 L1305100

From Trafalgar Square, Pall Mall East leads into Pall Mall, which runs from Haymarket to St James's Street, skirting St James's Square. The name of the street derives from 'paille maille', a mallet-and-ball game that was played in the area in the 17th century.

St James's Square features a bronze statue of King William III (1688-1702) in Classical style as a Roman general on horseback. An unusual feature of the statue is a molehill beneath the horse's hooves – William III died as a result of falling from his horse when it stumbled over a molehill, causing his enemies to toast 'the Little Gentleman in Black Velvet' – the mole that created the fatal hummock.

Chatham House at Number 10 St James's Square, now the headquarters of The Royal Institute of International Affairs, was once the home of William Ewart Gladstone, the 19th-century statesman and Prime Minister. An interesting feature of the house is the pair of inverted metal cones adorning the posts on either side of the front entrance steps. In past times, pedestrians used 'links', or torches, to light their way home at night, and extinguished them in these cones before going into the house.

St James's Palace in the St James's area is one of London's oldest palaces. It was commissioned by Henry VIII in the 16th century and constructed in Tudor style in red brick around four courtyards. King Charles II restored the palace in the 1660s after his restoration to the throne following the Civil War, and it became the principal residence of the monarch in London in 1698, after Whitehall Palace was destroyed by fire. At this time it also became the administrative centre and 'official residence' of the monarchy, a role it still retains, although it is no longer a royal residence. As the most senior royal palace in the UK it gives its name to the Royal Court, 'the Court of St James's'. The photograph on the opposite page shows the main entrance to St James's Palace, the gatehouse.

LONDON, ST JAMES'S PALACE c1900 L130355

LONDON, ADMIRALTY ARCH AND THE MALL c1965 L1305195

This elevated view shows the Mall, which forms an expansive and formal approach to Buckingham Palace from Trafalgar Square. Buckingham Palace, seen in the centre distance, is screened from Trafalgar Square by Admiralty Arch, built as part of the memorial scheme to Queen Victoria (died 1901) that was commissioned by her son and successor, Edward VII. In the background a little to the right of the Mall is the top of the Duke of York Column, which commemorates Prince Frederick (1763–1827), a son of George III, who was the Commander-in-Chief of the British Army during the French Revolutionary and Napoleonic Wars between 1789 and 1815. Prince Frederick, who had a disastrous military career, was the 'Grand Old Duke of York' of nursery rhyme fame who marched ten thousand men 'to the top of the hill, and he marched them down again'. Prince Frederick stands on top of his column at a height of 124 feet (about 38 metres) – legend says that he was placed so high to keep him away from his creditors!

At the western end of the Mall is Buckingham Palace, the British monarch's principal London home and the setting for state occasions and royal hospitality for foreign dignitaries. Buckingham Palace was originally Buckingham House, built in the early 1700s as the town house for the Duke of Buckingham. In 1761 King George III acquired the property for Queen Charlotte to use as a private retreat, and it became known as The Queen's House. It became the official residence of the monarch on the accession of Queen Victoria in 1837, thereafter known as Buckingham Palace.

Buckingham Palace is owned by the State and is not the monarch's personal property, unlike other royal residences such as Windsor Castle in Berkshire and Sandringham in Norfolk. The lavishly decorated state rooms of Buckingham Palace are open to the public each year for most of August and September, when visitors can view the Throne Room, Green Drawing Room, Silk Tapestry Rooms, Picture Gallery, State Dining Room, Blue Drawing Room, Music Room and White Drawing Room. Also open to visitors is the Queen's Gallery, where a changing exhibition of works of art and treasures from the royal collection are on display, which are kept in trust by the monarch for the nation.

As well as being the monarch's principal London residence, Buckingham Palace also houses the offices of the Royal Household, and around 450 people work there.

The front of Buckingham Palace is guarded by a detachment of Foot Guards, dressed in full dress uniform of red tunics and 'bearskins' – tall fur caps. The Foot Guards are drawn from five regiments, the Grenadier Guards, Coldstream Guards, Irish Guards, Scots Guards and Welsh Guards. The Changing of the Guard is a colourful event that takes place at 11.30 am on a daily basis from May to July, and on alternate dates throughout the rest of the year, when the New Guard parades along the Mall towards Buckingham Palace to replace the Old Guard, accompanied by music played by a military band.

LONDON, BUCKINGHAM PALACE c1890 L130173

LONDON, REGENT STREET c1890 L130079

The streets, squares and terraces of fine houses of the West End were developed in the late 17th, 18th and early 19th centuries. Regent Street was designed and built by John Nash between 1811 and 1825, and is seen in this photograph in 1890, just before all Nash's buildings except for All Souls' Church were replaced in the redevelopment that took place between 1895 and 1927, although the street still follows his original layout.

The name of Piccadilly in the West End probably derives from a tailor called Robert Baker who made a fortune selling stiff lace collars called 'picadils', which were very fashionable in the late 16th and early 17th centuries. Around 1612 he used his wealth to build a fine country house near what is now Piccadilly Circus, which locals nicknamed 'Piccadilly Hall'. At 181 Piccadilly is the famous Fortnum & Mason store, founded as a high-class grocery business by William Fortnum and Hugh Mason in 1707. On the frontage of the store is a huge clock which features mechanical models of Mr Fortnum and Mr Mason; every hour, when the clock chimes and plays 18th-century music, the two figures emerge and bow to each other.

The junction of Piccadilly Circus was formed in 1819 as one of the two links that joined together the three sections of John Nash's Regent Street; it was originally known as 'Regent Circus South' (with what is now Oxford Circus being then known as 'Regent Circus North'). The famous fountain in the middle of Piccadilly Circus with its statue depicting Eros, the Greek god of love, was erected as a memorial to the philanthropic nobleman Lord Shaftesbury who died in 1886. It was designed by Sir Alfred Gilbert, who had planned for the statue to represent the Angel of Christian Charity, not Eros, which many critics at the time felt was inappropriate. Sir Alfred Gilbert was so annoyed by the way that the memorial committee modified the statue from his original design that he refused to attend the unveiling of the fountain in 1893.

LONDON, PICCADILLY CIRCUS c1895 L130081

LONDON, MARBLE ARCH c1915 L130205

Hyde Park extends westwards from Piccadilly. A feature of Hyde
Park is Rotten Row, a sandy track maintained as a place to ride
horses. The name of Rotten Row comes from the French 'route du
roi', meaning 'route of the king', because it was set out during the
reign of King William III (1688-1702) who moved to Nottingham
House in Kensington, now Kensington Palace, in 1689 to enjoy the
clean 'country' air. Marble Arch was placed at the northern end of
Park Lane, at its junction with Oxford Street and Edgware Road, in
1851 to form an entrance into the north-east corner of Hyde Park.
Designed by John Nash, it was originally built on the Mall in 1827
as a gateway to Buckingham Palace. The statue of King George IV
that was intended for the top of Marble Arch now stands in Trafalgar
Square (see page 22). Inside Marble Arch are three small rooms which
were used as a police station until 1950, first by the royal constables
of Hyde Park, and later by the Metropolitan Police.

Another of London's monumental arches stands at the other end of Park Lane, where it converges with Knightsbridge, Piccadilly, Grosvenor Place and Constitution Hill at Hyde Park Corner. This is the Wellington Arch, also known as the Constitution Arch because it stands on Constitution Hill. Designed by Decimus Burton, it was built in 1826 to celebrate the Duke of Wellington's victory over Napoleonic forces at the battle of Waterloo in 1815. The arch of this impressive monument was originally crowned by Matthew Cotes Wyatt's magnificent bronze statue of the Duke of Wellington seated on his horse, Copenhagen. In 1885, when the French wars were long forgotten, the colossal statue was dismantled and transported to Aldershot, the home of the British Army, where it was re-erected on Round Hill. In 1912 the dramatic bronze by Adrian Jones that is seen in this photograph was erected on the arch, an allegorical rendering of Peace descending on the Quadriga (chariot) of War. It is the largest bronze statue in Britain.

**LONDON, THE WELLINGTON ARCH
HYDE PARK CORNER 1915**   L130202

On the western side of Hyde Park is Kensington Gardens, which features a statue beside the Long Water of the playwright James Barrie's most famous character, 'Peter Pan'; placed here in 1912, it was the gift of Barrie, who lived nearby and often walked his dog in the gardens. It was there that he met the Llewellyn Davies boys, George and Jack, who inspired him into writing about a baby boy (based on their baby brother Peter) who had magical adventures in Kensington Gardens, which eventually became the story of 'Peter Pan'. South of Hyde Park and Kensington Gardens is the exclusive district of Knightsbridge where the famous Harrods store stands on a five-acre site in Brompton Road – it is the largest department store in Europe. In 1898, Harrods was the first place in Britain to install a 'moving staircase'; customers disconcerted by this novel experience were offered a glass of brandy when they reached the top, to settle their nerves!

South of Knightsbridge is Chelsea, bounded to the south by the River Thames. The Royal Hospital Chelsea is a retirement home for British soldiers unfit for further duty due to injury or old age. It was founded by King Charles II in 1681, traditionally at the behest of his mistress Nell Gwynn after she met an old wounded soldier reduced to begging for charity. The residents of the Hospital are popularly known as 'Chelsea Pensioners'. The photograph on the opposite page shows Chelsea Pensioners on Oak Apple Day, 29th May. After his defeat at the battle of Worcester in 1651, during the Civil War, King Charles II hid in an oak tree from Parliamentarian forces. The tree protected him from discovery, and he managed to escape abroad. He was restored to the throne in 1660 and Oak Apple Day became a public holiday. It is celebrated as Founder's Day by the Chelsea Pensioners, and they are seen here posing in front of the statue of Charles II in the Figure Court of the Hospital, which has been decked with oak leaves for the occasion.

LONDON, CHELSEA PENSIONERS ON OAK APPLE DAY c1900 L130320

We now follow the Thames eastwards from Chelsea to Vauxhall Bridge, which is adorned with 4 statues by Alfred Drury and 4 by Frederick Pomeroy, representing the Arts and Sciences. On the south side of the bridge is Alfred Drury's statue representing Architecture. She holds a small model of St Paul's Cathedral in her hand, which the watermen of the Thames called 'Little St Paul's on the Water'. The statue is hidden in a niche on the bridge, and is only visible from the river banks or from river boat traffic passing under the bridge. Past Vauxhall Bridge on the north bank is the Tate Gallery, now known as Tate Britain, containing the UK's national collection of British art from 1500 to the present day. It opened in 1897, built on the site of the Millbank Prison, and the cost of its construction was covered by the sugar refiner Sir Henry Tate of Tate & Lyle fame, after whom the gallery was named. There is now a further branch of the Tate in London, Tate Modern, housed in the former Bankside Power Station in Southwark, which holds a collection of international modern art from 1900 to the present day.

LONDON, THE HOUSES OF PARLIAMENT 1908 L130149

We now follow the Thames downriver past Lambeth Bridge to the Palace of Westminster on the north bank, also known as the Houses of Parliament. The massive building was constructed between 1836 and 1860 in Victorian Gothic style to Sir Charles Barry's design, although its intricate ornament and detailing were conceived and wrought by Augustus Pugin. The monumental clock tower, surmounted by a richly-decorated belfry and spire, was designed by E B Denison. The name 'Big Ben' is popularly used to describe the clock tower together with its clock and bell, but is more correctly just the name of the Great Bell of the tower, which sounds the hour. The Great Bell was installed in 1858 and was probably named 'Big Ben in honour of Sir Benjamin Hall, the Commissioner of Works for the project, whose name is inscribed on it. Westminster Bridge spans the Thames between the Houses of Parliament and Lambeth on the south bank. It is painted green to echo the colour of the leather seats in the House of Commons on the side of the Palace of Westminster nearest the bridge.

On the Lambeth side of the Thames, and facing the Palace of Westminster, is St Thomas' Hospital, famous for its connection with the nursing pioneer Florence Nightingale. Her revolutionary school of nursing was established at this hospital in the 1860s and is still there, now known as The Florence Nightingale School of Nursing and Midwifery. The Florence Nightingale Museum in the hospital tells the story of her experiences in the military hospitals of the Crimean War of the 1850s, and her life's work campaigning to make nursing a respectable profession and to improve hospital facilities. South of the hospital is Lambeth Palace, seen in the photograph below, which is the official residence of the Archbishop of Canterbury, the head of the Church of England. To the right of the photograph is Lambeth's former parish church of St-Mary-at-Lambeth. The churchyard is the burial place of the two John Tradescants, father and son, famous gardeners, botanists and plant collectors of the 17th century. In 1979 the Tradescant Trust converted the redundant church into the Museum of Garden History.

LONDON, LAMBETH PALACE FROM THE SUSPENSION BRIDGE c1900 L130139

East of Lambeth is the Elephant and Castle area, a busy road junction named after the Elephant and Castle Inn. Both the inn and the road junction now look very different from this 1880s' view. In the middle of the northern roundabout of the modern road junction is a huge steel box-like structure which is a memorial to the scientist Michael Faraday, one of the pioneers of electricity, who was born in nearby Newington Butts in 1791. A listed building, it also houses the power plant and equipment for the London Underground Bakerloo line. Another famous person from this part of London was Charlie Chaplin, born into poverty in the Kennington area in 1889. His father deserted the family when Charlie was young and his mother spent much time in mental asylums, causing Charlie to be placed in the Lambeth workhouse and the Central London District School for paupers in Hanwell. He began his stage career in 1903 and eventually moved to America to become a star of the silver screen, but he never forgot his roots and returned in the 1950s to visit his former homes in Pownall Terrace (now Kennington Road) and Methley Street.

LONDON, THE ELEPHANT AND CASTLE 1885 L130028

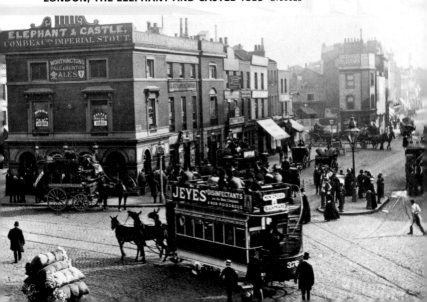

LONDON, SOUTHWARK, THE GEORGE INN c1875 L130130

Borough High Street in Southwark used to be lined with inns for it was an important route in medieval times, leading to London Bridge and the City of London in one direction and the pilgrimage destination of Canterbury in the other. In Chaucer's 'The Canterbury Tales', the pilgrims set out from the Tabard Inn at Southwark, and it was the landlord's idea that they should each tell a tale to entertain the others on their journey. Now gone, the Tabard Inn was located next to the historic George Inn which still stands off Borough High Street. London's only surviving galleried inn, it was originally built round three sides of a courtyard, and the inn's guests would stand on its galleries to watch performances by troupes of actors. William Shakespeare lived at Southwark for some time, and may have come here to see his plays performed. Now you can watch his plays in the wonderful Globe Theatre, a reconstruction of the open-air theatre built for Shakespeare's company, the Lord Chamberlain's Men, in the early 17th century, which stands on the south bank of the Thames at Bankside, near Southwark Bridge.

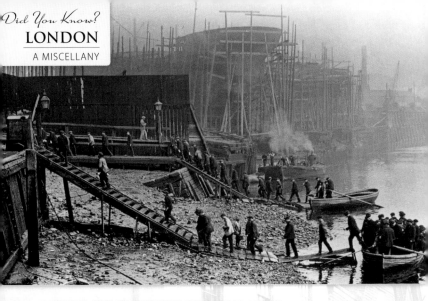

LONDON, THAMES SHIPBUILDING c1910 L130056

From Southwark, London Bridge crosses the Thames to the City of London and forms the western end of the 'Pool of London', the original part of the Port of London. The 'Upper Pool' is the section between London Bridge and Tower Bridge, and the 'Lower Pool' is from Tower Bridge to the Cherry Garden Pier in Rotherhithe. From the late 18th century, when London's docks began to be developed on a major scale, until the 1980s, when London's dockland trade came to an end (see page 44), many people living in the East End were employed in the extensive docks of the Pool of London as well as the shipbuilding yards which once dotted the eastern banks of the Thames; these included the great Millwall Yard, which launched, among others, Brunel's 'Great Eastern' in 1857. In this photograph, carpenters, coopers and ropemakers are arriving by boat to begin the day's toil at one of the shipbuilding yards. They clamber up the rickety steps to stake their claim to work – most were poorly-paid casual workers hired daily. In crisis by 1900, the last shipbuilding yards in London closed a few years after this photograph was taken.

All along this part of the Thames in the past, and powerfully described in the 19th century by Charles Dickens in his books, houses, riverside houses, tenements and inns tottered and decayed in places such as Deptford, Wapping and Shadwell. You can get an idea of what a riverside inn from that time was like by visiting the Prospect of Whitby pub in Wapping, next to the Pelican Stairs which lead down to the foreshore of the river. This hostelry was once known as The Devil's Tavern because of its notorious reputation – it was the haunt of shady characters who sold bodies washed up by the Thames to the medical schools for anatomical research – but was renamed The Prospect of Whitby after the name of a ship that transported coal to London from Newcastle which used to berth alongside the pub.

There is a gruesome reminder of crime and punishment in the past on the foreshore of the Thames outside The Prospect of Whitby pub at Wapping, in the form of a gibbet and hangman's noose. This recalls the old Execution Dock gibbet where criminals such as pirates, smugglers and mutineers who had committed crimes at sea and had been sentenced to death by the Admiralty courts, which had jurisdiction over water-borne crimes, were hanged from a gibbet constructed close to the low water mark of the tidal estuary of the Thames. Their bodies would be left dangling on the gibbet until they had been submerged by three high tides of the river. Executions took place here for over 400 years, until 1830. The actual site of the Execution Dock was nearer to another historic waterfront pub at Wapping, The Town of Ramsgate, located west of the Prospect and next to Old Wapping Stairs, another set of historic steps leading down to the waterfront. It was here that fishermen from Ramsgate in Kent used to sell their catch, hence the name of the pub.

LONDON, TOWER BRIDGE 1896 L130248

Tower Bridge, near the Tower of London, opened in 1894. It is a combined suspension and lifting bridge, and its bascules carrying the roadway can be fully raised to allow shipping to pass through. On 28th December 1952 a double-decker bus was being driven over the bridge just as the bascules began to rise. The driver managed to 'leap' the bus across the three feet drop to land it safely on the bascule on the other side, and it continued on its journey! In the foreground of this photograph is the Pool of London, seen here busy with barges and sailing ships in 1896. London's vast docks, on the north and south banks of the Thames east of the Tower, flourished from 1799 until finally closing in 1981, when their trade moved east, to the vast container port of Tilbury and other more accessible ports for modern shipping like Sheerness. Their sites have been redeveloped into the Docklands area of waterside flats, warehouse conversions and office buildings. The most famous building, the gigantic office tower of Canary Wharf, was started in 1987, and has now been joined by others.

This view looks across to Canary Wharf from south of the Thames, over the complex of historic buildings at Greenwich which is a World Heritage site. They include the National Maritime Museum, the 17th-century Queen's House, designed by Inigo Jones for Queen Anne, wife of King James I, which was the model for the White House in America, home of the President of the USA (centre foreground), and the Old Royal Naval College, originally the Seamen's Hospital founded by King William III and Queen Mary II in 1694 (the building with two domes). A feature of the Old Royal Naval College is the magnificent painted ceiling in the Great Hall by Sir James Thornhill, which took him nineteen years to complete in the early 1700s – he was paid by the yard for the work. Also at Greenwich is Flamsteed House, the Royal Observatory from 1675 until 1948 and the location of the Prime Meridian (the line of longitude at which the longitude is defined to be 0°) and Greenwich Mean Time; the time ball on its roof still drops at 1pm so that sailors on the Thames can set their clocks.

GREENWICH, THE VIEW FROM GREENWICH PARK TOWARDS CANARY WHARF 2005 G204706

SPORTING LONDON

Since 1924, Wembley Stadium in north-west London has been the home of the English national football team. The current stadium was built on the site of the famous old 'Twin Towers' stadium, and opened in 2007 with a capacity of 90,000. It has a partly retractable roof and is spanned by the huge Wembley Arch, the longest single span roof structure in the world. Wembley Stadium is the venue for the FA Cup final and also rugby league's Challenge Cup final. The national rugby union stadium is at Twickenham in south-west London, with a capacity of 84,000. London also has two Test cricket grounds, at Lord's in St John's Wood (home of Middlesex CCC) and The Oval in Kennington (home of Surrey CCC).

One of the most famous and prestigious tennis tournaments in the world takes place every summer in London's south-west suburb of Wimbledon, at the All England Tennis Club. The Championships, Wimbledon has been held since 1877 and is the oldest tennis tournament in the world. It is one of the four Grand Slam tennis tournaments (the other three Majors being the Australian Open, French Open and US Open) but is now unique for being the only one still played on grass, the original surface that gave the game of lawn tennis its name.

A highlight of London's year is the London Marathon each spring, in which around 35,000 runners follow a 26.2 miles (42.2 km) course around the city. The first London Marathon was held in 1981, and it is now one of the five top world marathons that that make up the World Marathon Majors competition. Set over a course around the River Thames, the race begins at three separate points around Blackheath and finishes in The Mall. It is both a serious racing event and a celebratory sporting festival in which many participants take part in fancy dress. Over the years the runners have raised huge amounts of money for charity – in fact, the London Marathon holds the Guinness world record as the largest annual fund raising event in the world. The first wheelchair marathon race was held in 1983, and this is now a significant part of the event.

London is the venue for the Oxford and Cambridge Boat Race each spring, rowed upstream on the Thames over a course of 4 miles and 374 yards (6.779 km) between Putney and Mortlake in south-west London. The race is contested by two teams of competing eights made up of students from the Boat Clubs of Oxford and Cambridge Universities. The first Boat Race was rowed in 1829 and it is now a major sporting event, attracting hundreds of thousands of spectators along the banks of the Thames to watch the action.

London has hosted the Summer Olympics twice, in 1908 and 1948. When it hosts the Summer Olympic and Paralympic Games in 2012, it will become the first city in the world to host the Summer Olympics three times.

Many sports are played in London, and far too many to outline here, but the city is particularly known for the five football clubs of Arsenal, Chelsea, Fulham, Tottenham Hotspur and West Ham United. They are all successful clubs, both at home and in Europe, and for various reasons they have all earned a place in football history, but West Ham fans can claim with some justification that the Hammers played a major part in England's World Cup victory in 1966 – three West Ham players were in the team that won the final, including the captain, Bobby Moore, and the two goal-scorers, Martin Peters and Geoff Hurst, who scored the first, and so far still the only, hat-trick in a World Cup final. A statue of the three, accompanied by fellow national team-member and Everton player Ray Wilson, stands in Barking Road opposite the Boleyn Arms, a short distance from West Ham's Boleyn Ground stadium at Upton Park.

EAST HAM, THE CHAMPIONS STATUE 2003 F6025

Did You Know?

LONDON
A MISCELLANY

QUIZ QUESTIONS

Answers on page 52.

1. Which London institution is known as 'The Old Lady of Threadneedle Street'?

2. Which character from a famous musical stage play and feature film was a flower girl in London's Covent Market?

3. A trip on the giant Ferris wheel known as the London Eye in one of its 'pods' is a great way to view the city. How many pods are there on the London Eye, and why is this number significant?

4. Who were known as 'mudlarks' in London in the past?

5. What in London is known as 'Cleopatra's Needle', and where will you find it?

6. Number 10 Downing Street in Whitehall is the official residence of the Prime Minister – but do you know who lives at Number 11 Downing Street?

7. Which famous fictional character lived at number 221b Baker Street in Marylebone?

8. Where would you end up if you took a train from 'Platform 9 ¾' at London's King's Cross Station?

9. Why was Sir Thomas Bloodworth (1620–1682) one of the worst Mayors of London the city has ever had?

10. One of London's distinctive modern buildings was voted the most admired new building in the world in 2005 – which was it?

LONDON, FLOWER SELLERS, COVENT GARDEN 1877 L130117

RECIPES

BOODLES ORANGE FOOL

The St James's area of central London is the location of a number of exclusive gentlemen's clubs such as the Reform, the Carlton and Boodle's. Boodle's Club was formed in the 1760s, and this luscious fool has been a speciality on the menu of its dining room for many years. It is a cross between a fool and a trifle, with a sponge cake base that soaks up the creamy, fruit-flavoured mixture on top.

> 4-6 trifle sponge cakes, cut into slices
>   about 1cm (½ inch) thick
> 300ml/ ½ pint double cream
> 50g/2oz caster sugar
> Grated rind and juice of 1 lemon
> Grated rind and juice of 2 oranges
> 2 or 3 orange slices or segments, and some long,
>   thin parings of orange rind, to decorate

Use the sponge cake slices to line the bottom and sides of a deep serving dish or bowl. Mix the orange and lemon rinds and juices with the sugar and stir until all the sugar has dissolved. In another bowl, whip the double cream until it just starts to thicken, then gradually whip in the sugar and fruit juice mixture, a little at a time, and continue to whip until the cream is light and thickened and all the juice is absorbed – do not overwhip the mixture though. Pour the cream mixture into the bowl, taking care not to dislodge the sponge slices. Cover the bowl with cling film and place it in the refrigerator to chill, for at least 2 hours, longer if possible, so that the juice can soak into the sponge slices and the cream thickens. When ready to serve, decorate the top of the fool with a few orange segments or slices, and a little thinly pared orange peel.

LONDON PARTICULAR

London used to be notorious for the dense fogs that covered the city in winter, a combination of mist and smoke from thousands of coal fires. The fogs are now a thing of the past, following the Clean Air Act of 1956, but are recalled in the name of this famous soup. The fogs were often called 'pea soupers', after the particularly thick soup that is made from dried peas, and Charles Dickens described the fog as a 'London Particular' in his novel 'Bleak House'; in time, the two names became interchangeable for both the fog and the pea soup. When making this soup, remember to put the peas to soak overnight in enough cold water to cover. This quantity will make enough for 4 people.

> 15g/ ½ oz butter
> 2 rashers streaky bacon, rinds removed,
>   chopped into pieces
> 1 onion, skinned and roughly chopped
> 1 carrot, trimmed and chopped
> 1 celery stick, chopped
> 225g/8oz split dried green or yellow peas,
>   soaked overnight in cold water
> 1.2 litres/2 pints chicken or ham stock
>   (ham stock is best to use if possible)
> Salt and pepper
> 1 teaspoonful Worcestershire sauce
> Garnish to serve – croutons, chopped grilled bacon,
>   or finely chopped fresh parsley

Melt the butter in a large saucepan. Add the chopped bacon, onion, carrot and celery and cook gently for 5-10 minutes, until beginning to soften. Drain the soaked peas and rinse them in cold running water, then add the peas to the pan. Add the stock, and bring to the boil. Reduce the heat, cover the pan with its lid and simmer gently for 1½ - 2 hours, until the peas are soft and mushy. Remove the pan from the heat and allow the soup to cool a little, then process the soup in a blender or liquidizer until it is smooth. Season the soup to taste with salt and pepper, and add the Worcestershire sauce. Reheat before serving. This is nice served with a garnish of a few croutons, or some grilled bacon, chopped into small pieces, or perhaps some finely chopped fresh parsley.

QUIZ ANSWERS

1. The Bank of England in Threadneedle Street has been known as 'The Old Lady of Threadneedle Street' since 1797, when a political cartoon by James Gillray appeared depicting the Prime Minister of the day, William Pitt the Younger, pretending to woo the Bank, personified by an elderly lady wearing a dress made of £1 notes sitting on a chest of gold. The cartoon was titled 'Political Ravishment or The Old Lady of Threadneedle Street in Danger', and this nickname for the bank stuck.

2. Eliza Doolittle, the heroine of the musical stage play 'My Fair Lady', which was filmed with Audrey Hepburn playing the lovable Cockney character.

3. There are 32 pods on the London Eye – representing the 32 London Boroughs.

4. Mudlarks were people who scavenged in the mud of the Thames at low tide, looking for items of value that they could sell. In the late 18th and 19th centuries many people living near the river made their living this way, especially youngsters, although it was a messy and unhealthy occupation. Nowadays, people searching the mud of the Thames for items of interest with metal detectors are also known as mudlarks.

5. Cleopatra's Needle is an Egyptian obelisk dating from 1500BC which was given to Britain by the Viceroy of Egypt and erected in 1878 on the Victoria Embankment, the north bank of the Thames between Westminster Bridge and Blackfriars Bridge.

6. Number 11 Downing Street is the official residence of the Second Lord of the Treasury, more commonly known nowadays as the Chancellor of the Exchequer.

7. Sherlock Holmes, the fictional detective created by Sir Arthur Conan Doyle, lived at 221b Baker Street in Marylebone. This address did not actually exist in Sherlock Holmes's 'era' (1881-1904), but now graces a building housing The Sherlock Holmes Museum.

8. The Hogwarts School of Witchcraft and Wizardry. 'Platform 9 ¾' at King's Cross Station is the fictional platform in the popular Harry Potter series of books, from where Harry Potter and his friends board the Hogwarts Express to the school. The platform is invisible to Muggle (non-magical) eyes, and is accessed by walking through the barrier between platforms 9 and 10. To capitalise on tourist interest in the connection between the station and the books, the site of the platform is marked by a sign, below which a luggage trolley appears to be disappearing into the wall.

9. The Great Fire of London of 1666 destroyed 13,200 houses, 87 parish churches and the old medieval St Paul's Cathedral. Fanned by a high wind, it raged through the wooden buildings of the old city for four days, partly due to the refusal of the Lord Mayor of London at that time, Sir Thomas Bloodworth, to allow houses to be demolished as a firebreak; his disparaging comment on the seriousness of the conflagration – 'Pish! A woman could piss it out' – has immortalised him as one of history's incompetents. Samuel Pepys recorded in his diary: 'People do all the world over cry out of the simplicity [stupidity] of my Lord Mayor … in this business of the fire, laying it all upon him.'

10. The building officially known as 30 St Mary Axe in London's financial district, popularly known as The Gherkin because of its resemblance to a giant vegetable. It was designed by Norman Foster and Arup engineers and completed in 2003. Perched in the City like a space rocket about to take off, it is a distinctive feature of the modern skyline and greatly admired by architects around the world. The building was awarded the 2004 RIBA Stirling Prize, with the judges reaching a unanimous decision for the first time in the prestigious prize's history, and in 2005 it was voted the most admired new building in the world in a survey of the world's largest architectural firms, published in the 2006 edition of the 'BD World Architecture 200'.

FRANCIS FRITH

PIONEER VICTORIAN PHOTOGRAPHER

Francis Frith, founder of the world-famous photographic archive, was a complex and multi-talented man. A devout Quaker and a highly successful Victorian businessman, he was philosophical by nature and pioneering in outlook. By 1855 he had already established a wholesale grocery business in Liverpool, and sold it for the astonishing sum of £200,000, which is the equivalent today of over £15,000,000. Now in his thirties, and captivated by the new science of photography, Frith set out on a series of pioneering journeys up the Nile and to the Near East.

INTRIGUE AND EXPLORATION

He was the first photographer to venture beyond the sixth cataract of the Nile. Africa was still the mysterious 'Dark Continent', and Stanley and Livingstone's historic meeting was a decade into the future. The conditions for picture taking confound belief. He laboured for hours in his wicker dark-room in the sweltering heat of the desert, while the volatile chemicals fizzed dangerously in their trays. Back in London he exhibited his photographs and was 'rapturously cheered' by members of the Royal Society. His reputation as a photographer was made overnight.

VENTURE OF A LIFE-TIME

By the 1870s the railways had threaded their way across the country, and Bank Holidays and half-day Saturdays had been made obligatory by Act of Parliament. All of a sudden the working man and his family were able to enjoy days out, take holidays, and see a little more of the world.

With typical business acumen, Francis Frith foresaw that these new tourists would enjoy having souvenirs to commemorate their days out. For the next thirty years he travelled the country by train and by pony and trap, producing fine photographs of seaside resorts and beauty spots that were keenly bought by millions of Victorians. These prints were painstakingly pasted into family albums and pored over during the dark nights of winter, rekindling precious memories of summer excursions. Frith's studio was soon supplying retail shops all over the country, and by 1890 F Frith & Co had become the greatest specialist photographic publishing company in the world, with over 2,000 sales outlets, and pioneered the picture postcard.

FRANCIS FRITH'S LEGACY

Francis Frith had died in 1898 at his villa in Cannes, his great project still growing. By 1970 the archive he created contained over a third of a million pictures showing 7,000 British towns and villages.

Frith's legacy to us today is of immense significance and value, for the magnificent archive of evocative photographs he created provides a unique record of change in the cities, towns and villages throughout Britain over a century and more. Frith and his fellow studio photographers revisited locations many times down the years to update their views, compiling for us an enthralling and colourful pageant of British life and character.

We are fortunate that Frith was dedicated to recording the minutiae of everyday life. For it is this sheer wealth of visual data, the painstaking chronicle of changes in dress, transport, street layouts, buildings, housing and landscape that captivates us so much today, offering us a powerful link with the past and with the lives of our ancestors.

Computers have now made it possible for Frith's many thousands of images to be accessed almost instantly. The archive offers every one of us an opportunity to examine the places where we and our families have lived and worked down the years. Its images, depicting our shared past, are now bringing pleasure and enlightenment to millions around the world a century and more after his death.

For further information visit: www.francisfrith.com

INTERIOR DECORATION

Frith's photographs can be seen framed and as giant wall murals in thousands of pubs, restaurants, hotels, banks, retail stores and other public buildings throughout Britain. These provide interesting and attractive décor, generating strong local interest and acting as a powerful reminder of gentler days in our increasingly busy and frenetic world.

FRITH PRODUCTS

All Frith photographs are available as prints and posters in a variety of different sizes and styles. In the UK we also offer a range of other gift and stationery products illustrated with Frith photographs, although many of these are not available for delivery outside the UK – see our web site for more information on the products available for delivery in your country.

THE INTERNET

Over 100,000 photographs of Britain can be viewed and purchased on the Frith web site. The web site also includes memories and reminiscences contributed by our customers, who have personal knowledge of localities and of the people and properties depicted in Frith photographs. If you wish to learn more about a specific town or village you may find these reminiscences fascinating to browse. Why not add your own comments if you think they would be of interest to others? See **www.francisfrith.com**

PLEASE HELP US BRING FRITH'S PHOTOGRAPHS TO LIFE

Our authors do their best to recount the history of the places they write about. They give insights into how particular towns and villages developed, they describe the architecture of streets and buildings, and they discuss the lives of famous people who lived there. But however knowledgeable our authors are, the story they tell is necessarily incomplete.

Frith's photographs are so much more than plain historical documents. They are living proofs of the flow of human life down the generations. They show real people at real moments in history; and each of those people is the son or daughter of someone, the brother or sister, aunt or uncle, grandfather or grandmother of someone else. All of them lived, worked and played in the streets depicted in Frith's photographs.

We would be grateful if you would give us your insights into the places shown in our photographs: the streets and buildings, the shops, businesses and industries. Post your memories of life in those streets on the Frith website: what it was like growing up there, who ran the local shop and what shopping was like years ago; if your workplace is shown tell us about your working day and what the building is used for now. Read other visitors' memories and reconnect with your shared local history and heritage. With your help more and more Frith photographs can be brought to life, and vital memories preserved for posterity, and for the benefit of historians in the future.

Wherever possible, we will try to include some of your comments in future editions of our books. Moreover, if you spot errors in dates, titles or other facts, please let us know, because our archive records are not always completely accurate—they rely on 140 years of human endeavour and hand-compiled records. You can email us using the contact form on the website.

Thank you!

For further information, trade, or author enquiries
please contact us at the address below:

**The Francis Frith Collection, Oakley Business Park,
Wylye Road, Dinton, Wiltshire SP3 5EU.**
Tel: +44 (0)1722 716 376   Fax: +44 (0)1722 716 881
e-mail: sales@francisfrith.co.uk   **www.francisfrith.com**